KU-693-632

SUDDENLY SENIOR

The Funny Thing About Getting Older

· TOM HAY

ILLUSTRATIONS BY IAN BAKER

summersdale

SUDDENLY SENIOR

Summersdale Publishers Ltd
46 West Street
Chichester
West Sussex
PO19 1RP
UK

www.summersdale.com

Printed and bound in India

ISBN: 978-1-84953-076-7

Substantial discounts on bulk quantities of Summersdale books are available to corporations, professional associations and other organisations. For details contact Summersdale Publishers by telephone: +44 (0) 1243 771107, fax: +44 (0) 1243 786300 or email: nicky@summersdale.com.

Contents

Editor's Note...5

Achy Breaky Parts...7

Hair-um Scare 'Em...24

The Sounds of Silence..32

Sight, for Sore Eyes...41

Biting Back...50

Medication's Whatcha Need...59

Stayin' Alive...67

Holding Back the Years..75

Love Me Tender...89

Relight My Fire..99

Old-fashioned Romance...110

Last Innings...121

Driving Miss Daisy..128

Partial Recall...136

Old Folks, at Home..146

The Gift of Grandkids..156

And Another Thing…..163

Keeping a Twinkle in Your Wrinkle..............................180

A Word to the Wizened..200

Editor's Note

We're old enough to have seen life begin at forty. Perhaps we've faced the big five-O with a frolic and seen in our sixtieth with a smile. Officially attaining senior citizen status and being awarded a free bus pass might seem to some the last landmark celebration to be enjoyed in later life.

But, having wrestled with middle age, we must remember that from here on in it's all downhill in the nicest possible way; a time to kick back, relax and, in the words of William Shakespeare, 'With mirth and laughter let old wrinkles come.'

This book, a hearty tonic of wit, wisdom and wisecracks, will help you keep a spring in your step and a song in your heart (albeit a golden oldie), giving you a (somewhat creaky) leg-up to enjoying the brighter side of feeling suddenly senior. So read on and, as you do, don't be too alarmed when you start to feel a twinkle in your wrinkle!

ACHY BREAKY PARTS

I'm at an age where my back
goes out more than I do.

Phyllis Diller

One morning, while lying in bed, an elderly man leans over to kiss his wife when all of a sudden she shouts, 'Don't touch me – I'm dead!'
'What are you talking about?' says the husband.
'I'm definitely dead,' replies the wife.
'What in the world makes you think you're dead?'
'I woke up this morning and nothing hurts!'

I don't need you to remind me of my age. I have a bladder to do that for me.

Stephen Fry

As for me, except for an occasional heart attack, I feel as young as I ever did.

Robert Benchley

Like a lot of fellows around here, I have a furniture problem. My chest has fallen into my drawers.

Billy Casper

An old fellow meets the woman of his dreams. When he plucks up the courage to propose, he gets down on one knee and tells her there are two things he would like to ask. 'First,' he says, 'will you marry me?' The woman replies, 'Yes! Yes, I will!' and awaits his second question eagerly. 'That's wonderful!' he cries. 'Now for my second question: will you help me up?'

An aging gent visits his doctor for a check up. A few days later the doctor sees him walking along the street with a stunning young lady on his arm. A week passes and, on his follow-up visit, the doctor says to the man, 'You're doing well, aren't you?'

'Just doing what you told me to, doc,' the patient replies. 'Get a hot mama and be cheerful.'

'Actually, I said, "You've got a heart murmur, be careful".'

A recently retired gentleman applies for his state pension. After waiting in line for quite a long time, he arrives at the counter. The clerk asks him for his identification to verify his age. The man looks in his pockets and realises he has left his wallet at home. 'Will I have to go home and come back?' he asks. The woman pauses and then says, 'Unbutton your shirt please, sir.' The man opens his shirt, revealing lots of curly silver hair. The woman says, 'That silver hair on your chest is proof enough for me,' and processes his application. When he gets home, the man excitedly tells his wife about his experience, to which she replies, 'It's a good job you didn't take one of your blue pills before you went – if she'd asked to see any more of you she'd never have believed you're sixty-five!'

They say that age is all in your mind. The trick is keeping it from creeping down into your body.

Anonymous

I don't deserve this award, but I have arthritis
and I don't deserve that either.

Jack Benny

An irate customer calls up her local
newsagent and demands to know why her
Sunday paper hasn't arrived. 'I'm sorry,
madam,' the newsagent calmly informs her,
'but I'm afraid today is Saturday. The Sunday
paper is not delivered until Sunday.' There is
a long pause on the other end of the phone,
before the lady replies, 'And I'll bet that's why
no one was in church today.'

I complain that the years fly past, but then
I look in a mirror and see that very few of
them actually got past.

Robert Brault

The problem with beauty is that it's like being born rich and getting poorer.

Joan Collins

A senior lady goes to the doctor complaining of a range of aches and pains. After examining her, the doctor feels he should be frank: 'Well, Mrs Smith, I'm sorry to say that the aches and pains you're getting are all part of the natural aging process. I'm afraid I can't prescribe anything to make you younger.' 'Well, doctor,' she replies, 'I'm not so worried about getting younger, I'd just like you to help make sure I get a little bit older!'

You know you're getting old when you can pinch an inch on your forehead.

John Mendoza

An aging playboy visits his doctor after a lifetime of wine, women and song. 'Well,' says the doctor. 'The good news is you don't have to give up singing'.

A senior man walks awkwardly into an ice cream shop and pulls himself slowly, painfully, up onto a stool. After catching his breath, he orders a banana split.
The waitress asks kindly, 'Crushed nuts today?'
'No,' he replies, 'Arthritis.'

After thirty, a body has a mind of its own.

Bette Midler

I was getting dressed and a peeping tom looked in the window, took a look and pulled down the shade.

Joan Rivers on getting old

A retired woman is complaining to her friend about the amount of housework she has to do: 'I spend all day washing, ironing, cleaning, doing the dishes...' she says. 'But what about your husband?' asks her friend. 'My husband? No – I make him wash himself.'

I don't feel old. I don't feel anything until noon. Then it's time for my nap.

Bob Hope

Alf and Vera, a couple in their sixties, are holidaying in America. Alf has always wanted some authentic American cowboy boots, so he treats himself to a pair. Back at the hotel, he puts them on and walks into the bedroom and says to his wife, 'Notice anything different about me?'

'No,' she replies, after looking him up and down. Frustrated, Alf storms off into the bathroom, undresses, and walks back into the room completely naked except for his beloved boots. Again he asks, a little louder this time, 'Notice anything different about me *now*?'

Vera looks him up and down and says, 'Alf, what's different? It's hanging down today, it was hanging down yesterday, it'll be hanging down again tomorrow!'

As you get older, the pickings get slimmer, but the people don't.

Carrie Fisher

I refuse to think of them as chin
hairs. I think of them as
stray eyebrows.

Janette Barber

I guess I don't mind so much being old, as I mind being fat and old.

Peter Gabriel

Early one evening, a police car pulls up in front of Grandma Rose's house. She looks out of her window and is shocked to see her husband being escorted out of the car by a police officer. She meets them at the door and is soon relieved to hear that her husband hasn't been up to mischief but had become lost while trying to find his way home from the pub.

'Oh, Stanley,' says Rose. 'You've been going to that pub for over thirty years! How could you get lost?' Leaning close to his wife, so that the policeman can't hear him, Stanley whispers, 'I wasn't lost. I was just too tired to walk home!'

A lady wearing a flowing dress and wide-brimmed hat quickly realises that she could have made a better choice of clothes for such a windy day.

As she's walking past a couple of policemen on the corner of her street, a gust of wind blows her hat off and catches her skirt, blowing it up to reveal she has no underwear on. The woman is promptly arrested for indecent exposure.

At the police station the chief constable says, 'Madam, what on earth were you thinking letting your skirt blow up, exposing yourself just to catch your hat?' To which the lady replies: 'That's easy. Everything under my skirt is seventy years old; that hat was brand new!'

As we grow older, our bodies get shorter and our anecdotes longer.

Robert Quillen

Time wounds all heels.

Dorothy Parker

Wrinkled was not one of the things I wanted
to be when I grew up.

Robert Frost

In a man's middle years there is scarcely a
part of the body he would hesitate to turn
over to the proper authorities.

E. B. White

A woman walks into a bar and orders a Scotch and two drops of water, 'It's my sixtieth birthday today,' she explains. The barman says, 'Well, since it's your birthday I'll buy you a drink.'

As the woman finishes her drink a woman to her right says, 'I guess I should buy you a drink too.' The birthday girl says, 'All right. I'll have a Scotch and two drops of water.'

As she finishes her drink, the man to her left says, 'Since I'm the only one that hasn't bought you a drink I guess I might as well buy you one too.' The woman says, 'OK, well make it another Scotch with two drops of water.' As the bartender gives her the drink he says, 'Madam, I'm dying of curiosity. Why the Scotch and only two drops of water?'

The woman replies, 'Well, when you're my age, you realise that you can hold your liquor but you certainly can't hold your water!'

HAIR-UM SCARE 'EM

I love bald men. Just because you've lost your fuzz don't mean you ain't a peach.

Dolly Parton

A man consults his friend about his increasing hair loss: 'I'm having to find more and more extravagant ways of combing my hair to make it look as if I have any left,' says one man. 'I know what you mean,' says a similarly balding man. 'I've seen men down-comb, up-comb and cross-comb. The thing is, you get to a stage where you only have three options left: parted, not parted, and departed.'

There's one thing about baldness; it's neat.

Don Herald

It's great to have a grey hair. Ask anyone who's bald.

Rodney Dangerfield

A balding gent walks into a barber shop and says, 'I'd like a haircut, please,' to which the hairdresser replies, 'Certainly, which one?'

There is more felicity on the far side of baldness
than young men can possibly imagine.

Logan Pearsall Smith

Two ladies in their sixties are discussing
an upcoming dance at their country club.
'I've been told that the dress code is to wear
something that matches our husband's hair,
so I'll be wearing my black, silky dress with
the silvery flecks!' says Mrs Smith with a
chortle. 'Oh my goodness,' says Mrs Jones,
thinking of her husband's bare noggin, 'I'd
better not go in that case; I don't want to
reveal *that* much!'

The whiter my hair becomes, the more ready
people are to believe what I say.

Bertrand Russell

There is only one cure for grey hair. It was invented by a Frenchman. It is called the guillotine.

P. G. Wodehouse

What should you buy if your hair begins falling out?
A good vacuum cleaner.

Grey hair is God's graffiti.

Bill Cosby

A man whose hair has long since departed the top of his head sits down in the barber's chair, feeling despondent.

He begins telling the barber about his bad experience at the hair transplant clinic: 'I thought, if it's good enough for Elton then it's good enough for me, but I couldn't stand the pain.' The man then brightens up when he comes up with a wager for the barber: 'If you can make my hair look like yours without causing me any discomfort, I'll pay you a thousand pounds.' The barber thinks about this for a moment, picks up his clippers and shaves his own head completely bare. 'That'll be one thousand pounds please, sir.'

I have a better head of hair than Rick Perry; it's just not in a place I can show you.

Kinky Friedman

My daughter teases me once in a while saying, 'Remember when you used to be my mother and you had black hair?'

Loni Anderson

They talk about the economy this year... my hairline is in recession, my waistline is in inflation. Altogether, I'm in a depression.

Rick Majerus

A hair in the head is worth two in the brush.

William Hazlitt

THE SOUNDS OF SILENCE

He needs to read lips. I don't mind him reading lips, but he uses one of those yellow highlighters.

Brian Kiley on his grandfather's hearing problems

A man goes to his doctor and says, 'I don't think my wife's hearing is as good as it used to be. What should I do?' The doctor replies, 'Try this test to find out for sure. When your wife is in the kitchen doing dishes, stand fifteen feet behind her and ask her a question, if she doesn't respond keep moving closer, asking the question until she hears you.'

The man goes home and sees his wife preparing dinner. He stands fifteen feet behind her and says, 'What's for dinner, honey?' He gets no response, so he moves to ten feet behind her and asks again. Still no response, so he moves to five feet. Again, no answer. Finally he stands directly behind her and says, 'Honey, what's for supper?' She replies, 'For the fourth time, I SAID CHICKEN!'

Gloria and her lifelong friends Sally and Janice are discussing their increasing memory loss over a cup of tea: 'I think I must be getting old,' confides Sally. 'I sometimes find myself at the foot of the stairs, and I can't remember if I was going up to get something or coming back down.'

'I know what you mean,' says Janice. 'The other day I was in front of the fridge and I couldn't remember if I was taking something out, or if I had just put something in.' Gloria sits up and reaches for a biscuit. 'Well,' she says, 'I haven't had any problems like that so far, knock on wood', rapping three times on the table. Suddenly, looking a little startled, she stands up. 'Excuse me,' she says, 'Was that someone knocking at the door?'

An aging gentleman is on the bus home from town, telling his friend about his new hearing aid: 'I've had hearing problems for years, as you know, so I thought it was about time I treated myself to a top-of-the-range hearing aid,' he says, pointing to the neat device in his ear. He continues, 'Eight hundred pounds it cost me... but it's worth it, it's absolutely perfect; I can hear the birds singing in the trees!'

'What kind is it?' his friend asks, looking suitably impressed.

'Oh, er... twelve thirty,' the man replies.

An older couple go to church one Sunday. Halfway through the service, the wife leans over and whispers in her husband's ear, 'I've just let out a silent fart. What do you think I should do?' Her husband replies, 'Put a new battery in your hearing aid, dear.'

Two young boys are spending the night at their grandparents' house. At bedtime, the two boys kneel beside their beds to say their prayers. The youngest one begins praying at the top of his lungs: 'I PRAY FOR A BICYCLE... I PRAY FOR A NEW COMPUTER... I PRAY FOR A NEW DVD PLAYER...' His older brother leans over, nudges him and says, 'Why are you shouting your prayers? God isn't deaf.' To which the little brother replies, 'No, but grandma is!'

One of the best hearing aids a man can have is an attentive wife.

Groucho Marx

An aging man decides it's time he invested in a hearing aid, but he feels a little reluctant to spend lots of money.

While investigating his options at the local hearing centre, the man asks, 'What price do your hearing aids start at?' To which the assistant replies, 'Our entry-level model is one hundred pounds, and our top of the line is five hundred.' The man considers this and still thinks the price is too much. 'Is there absolutely nothing cheaper?' he asks. 'Well,' the assistant says, 'I shouldn't really tell you this, but we do have some recovered models we could let you have for a small charge.' At this the man requests to see the cut-price model. 'You simply put this earpiece in and attach the wire to the inside of your pocket.' 'It seems a bit basic,' the man says, 'How does it work?'

'Well,' the assistant replies, 'for twenty pounds it doesn't work; but when people see you wearing it they'll start shouting at you anyway!'

Since I came to the White House, I got two hearing aids, a colon operation… and I was shot. The damn thing is I've never felt better in my life.

Ronald Reagan

Three old friends are out for an amble:
'Windy today, isn't it?' Geoff says.
No,' Cyril says, 'it's Thursday!'
Jim says, 'So am I. Let's go and get a pint.'

By deafness one gains in one respect more than one loses; one misses more nonsense than sense.

Horace Walpole

A senior lady is driving along the motorway, being careful to adhere to the speed limit and keep a safe distance from other cars. After a while she can see that a police car is behind her in the same lane. Feeling slightly self-conscious, she checks her speed and sees that she is well within the limit.

However, the policeman continues to follow her and after a while she notices he's switched his flashing lights on. The lady decides to pull over. The policeman walks up to her window and begins speaking. As he does this, the lady points to her ear and shakes her head, indicating that she is deaf. The policeman smiles and, knowing sign language, signs back, 'That's no problem, madam. I'm here to tell you that your horn is stuck!'

I would write plays for my grandmother, who was stone deaf, my mother and the dog; that was our audience.

Jayne Meadows

An elderly man decides that it has become necessary to invest in a hearing aid, and so visits a specialist, who gives him a device that restores his hearing completely.

After a month, the man goes back for a check-up: 'Your hearing is perfect,' the specialist says, 'your family must be really pleased that you can hear again.' To which the man replies, 'Well, I haven't actually told my family yet. I've just been sitting around and listening to their conversations... and considering what they've been saying about me I can see I've got some big changes to make to my will!'

SIGHT, FOR SORE EYES

The easiest way to diminish the appearance of wrinkles is to keep your glasses off when you look in the mirror.

Joan Rivers

David and Paula, a couple in their late sixties, are getting ready for bed. Paula is undressing in front of her full-length mirror, taking a long, hard look at herself.

'You know, David,' she comments, 'I stare into this mirror and I see an ancient creature. My face has more crows feet than a bird sanctuary, my boobs have gone south, my bingo wings are big enough for me to take off and my bum is starting to look like a hundred-year-old saddle bag. Darling, please tell me just one positive thing about my body so I can feel better about myself.'

David studies Paula critically for a moment and then says in a soft, thoughtful voice, 'Well, dear, there is at least one thing that's in good nick – there is absolutely nothing wrong with your eyesight!'

I was walking down the street wearing glasses when the prescription ran out.

Steven Wright

My face in the mirror isn't wrinkled
or drawn.
My house isn't dirty. The cobwebs are gone.
My garden looks lovely and so does my lawn.
I think I might never put my glasses back on.

Anonymous

I don't read anything any more. I don't have
the eyesight… I think I've read everything
that's worth reading.

John Gould

It's not what you look at that matters, it's
what you see.

Henry David Thoreau

I am getting to an age when I can only enjoy the last sport left. It is called hunting for your spectacles.

Edward Grey

Jack, a senior man, is giving his testimony in court. The defence lawyer asks Jack, 'Did you see my client commit this burglary?'

'Yes,' says Jack, 'I have no doubt it was him.' The lawyer, pressing Jack further, asks again: 'Now, Jack, this happened at night. Can you be entirely sure that it was my client you saw?'

'Yes,' says Jack, 'I saw him as plain as day.' Then the lawyer asks, 'Jack, with all due respect, at your age a man's eyesight isn't all that it used to be. Just how far can you see at night?' Jack says, 'Well, I can see the moon, how far is that?'

The grey-framed spectacles magnified the grey hazel eyes, but there was no greyness in the mind.

John Gunther

One day, Harry, a sporty man in his sixties, arrives home from an afternoon of golf, feeling depressed.

'I've decided I'm giving up golf. My eyesight has become so bad that once I've hit the ball, I can't see where it went.' His wife consoles him, makes him a nice cup of tea and says, 'Why don't you take our Arthur along next weekend and give it one more try?'

'That's no good,' sighs Harry. Your brother's ten years older than I am. He can't help.'

'He may be a bit older than you,' says the wife, 'but his eyesight has never been better.'

So the next weekend, Harry heads off to the golf course with his brother-in-law. He tees up, makes his shot, and looks down the fairway, squinting.

He turns to his brother-in-law and asks, 'Did you see the ball?'

'Of course!' replies Arthur. 'I have perfect eyesight.'

'Right – where did it go?' asks Harry.

'Oh, er, sorry... I don't remember.'

If you ever find happiness by hunting for it,
you will find it, as the old woman did her lost
spectacles, safe on her own nose all the time.

Josh Billings

To see what is in front of one's nose needs a
constant struggle.

George Orwell

A senior woman pays a visit to her local pharmacy to complain about a product she's been using regularly.

'I've been applying this every day for a month and it's just not working,' the woman says, presenting the tube to the pharmacist. The pharmacist takes the product and examines it. 'Well,' the pharmacist says, 'to my knowledge this is a very effective and reliable treatment.'

'I've been brushing with it twice a day,' the woman insists, 'once in the morning and once at night, and I can honestly say it has done me no good.'

'Well madam, there shouldn't really be any need to use a brush – haemorrhoid cream can be applied quite easily without one,' says the pharmacist, looking slightly alarmed. 'Ah…' the woman replies, 'I see. Could you do me a favour and check your records? I think I might be due for an eye examination.'

BITING BACK

I don't have false teeth. Do you
think I'd buy teeth like these?

Carol Burnett

A senior couple are enjoying a meal at a fine restaurant when all of a sudden the old man sneezes: 'I'm so proud of you,' his wife says, 'You've finally learned to put your hand in front of your mouth!'
'Of course I have,' her husband replies crossly, 'How the hell else am I going to catch my teeth?'

A boy visits his grandma with his mate. While the boy is talking to his grandma in the kitchen, his friend helps himself to some peanuts from a bowl. When it's time to go his friend calls out: 'Thanks for the peanuts!'
'That's all right,' the grandma replies. 'Since I lost my dentures I can only suck the chocolate off them!'

Laughter doesn't require teeth.

Bill Newton

A care home nurse brings her six-year-old daughter to work one day to have a look around. The little girl is fascinated by all the paraphernalia, such as the walkers, wheelchairs and gripping devices. They pay one lady a special visit, she has just got up and is yet to put her teeth in. The little girl's eyes widen in shock on seeing the full set of false teeth floating in a glass. She turns to her mum and whispers, 'The tooth fairy will never believe this!'

I told my dentist my teeth are going yellow. He told me to wear a brown tie.

Rodney Dangerfield

What's one thing that an old person can do
that a younger person can't?
Sing aloud whilst brushing their teeth!

An old couple are sitting down at a table in
a restaurant, waiting for their food to arrive.
The waiter sets down their meals and notices
a short while later that they are meticulously
splitting the food between the two of them.
Fair enough, he thinks, but then he notices
that the wife is just sitting there while the
husband is busily tucking in. He then asks
them if there's any problem with the food.
'Oh, no,' the old man says, 'it's just that
after fifty years of marriage we always split
everything down the middle.' Still a little
confused, the waiter then asks the lady if she's
going to eat, and she replies, 'Not yet. You
see, it's *his* turn with the teeth!'

After eating his dinner, an old man coughs violently, sending his false teeth flying across the room. 'Oh dear,' he says, 'they're ruined... smashed to bits. There's no way I can afford another set.'

'Don't worry, Dad,' says his son, 'I'll get a pair from my pal at work. Just give me what's left of your set so I can give him an idea of the size.' The next day the son comes back with the teeth, which fit perfectly. 'This is wonderful, son' says the man. 'Your friend must be a very good dentist.'

'Oh,' says the son, 'he's not a dentist, he's an undertaker.'

We idolised the Beatles [and] the Rolling Stones, who in those days still had many of their original teeth.

Dave Barry

The first thing I do in the morning is brush
my teeth and sharpen my tongue.

Dorothy Parker

While watching a movie at the cinema, an
elderly man begins rummaging around at
the feet of the people sitting next to him.
Becoming slightly annoyed at him, the lady in
the neighbouring seat whispers crossly, 'Just
what is it that you're doing down there?'
'I've lost a toffee,' the old man replies.
'You're going through all that bother just for
a toffee?' the woman asks.
'Yes,' says the old man, 'you see, my teeth
are in it.'

Two ladies, fiercely competitive in their latter years, are attending a dinner at their favourite country club. 'Well, Margaret,' one says, 'you're looking absolutely splendid tonight. And what's this?' she asks, noticing her necklace, 'Real pearls, I suppose?' 'Why yes, dear,' Margaret replies. 'Of course,' the other retorts, 'in order to tell for sure, I'd have to bite them, what?'
'I'd be perfectly happy for you to do that, dear,' Margaret says, 'except, you'd need real teeth for that, wouldn't you?'

She had so many gold teeth... she used to have to sleep with her head in a safe.

W. C. Fields

MEDICATION'S
WHATCHA NEED

Every time I hear it, I think I'm
supposed to put my breast in an
envelope and send it
to someone.

Jan King on the word 'mammogram'

A man in his sixties with a much younger wife decides to try Viagra so that he can keep up with her demands in the bedroom. They go to pick up his Viagra prescription, but the man baulks upon seeing the £5-per-pill price. His wife, on the other hand, looks indifferent… 'I don't know,' she says, 'thirty pounds a year isn't so bad.'

A hospital bed is a parked taxi with the meter running.

Groucho Marx

I'm taking Viagra and drinking prune juice – I don't know if I'm coming or going.

Rodney Dangerfield

An aging woman goes to her doctor to see what he can recommend for her troublesome constipation. 'It's terrible,' she says to the doctor. 'I haven't had a bowel movement in more than a week.'

'I see. Have you done anything about it?' asks the doctor.

'Oh, yes,' she replies, 'I sit in the bathroom for a good half an hour in the morning and then again at night.'

'No,' the doctor says, 'I mean do you take anything?'

'Of course I do,' she answers, 'I take the crossword book.'

A senior man is recovering from surgery when a nurse asks him how he is feeling.

'I'm OK but I didn't like the four-letter-word the doctor used in surgery,' he replies.

'What did he say?' asks the nurse, looking concerned.

'OOPS!' He exclaims.

A man comes home from work and notices his father has hidden himself behind the sofa. 'What's the problem?' he asks his dad. 'Are the children getting a bit too rowdy today?' The old man shakes his head and reaches into his trouser pocket for his prescription and points to the small print, 'Read the label,' he says, 'Take two pills a day. KEEP AWAY FROM CHILDREN.'

A retired gentleman goes to the doctor and tells him that he hasn't been feeling well. The doctor examines him, leaves the room, and comes back with three different bottles of pills. The doctor says, 'Take the green pill with a big glass of water when you get up. Take the blue pill with a big glass of water after lunch. Then just before going to bed, take the red pill with another big glass of water.' Startled to be put on so much medicine, the elderly man stammers, 'My goodness, exactly what's my problem?' The doctor says, 'You're not drinking enough water.'

A senior man is nervously awaiting the results of his medical when the doctor returns with his results. 'Well, doctor,' he says, 'how do I stand?'
'To be honest,' the doctor replies, 'that's what's puzzling me.'

An old man goes to the pharmacy for some cough syrup. The assistant can't find any so he recommends a strong laxative. The old man asks, 'How will a laxative help my congestion?'
'It won't,' replies the assistant, 'but you'll be too scared to cough.'

A woman is waiting at the pharmacy for her HRT prescription. As the pharmacist hands over her medicine, he makes a point of explaining the dosage directions: 'Now, Mrs Smith, it's important that you take no more than one tablet every four hours.' To which Mrs Smith replies, 'There'll be no problems there, I can assure you. It usually takes me at least two hours to find the bottle, and another two to get the damn lid off!'

Now I'm getting older I don't need to do drugs any more. I can get the same effect just by standing up real fast.

Jonathan Katz

You don't really know the meaning of embarrassment until your hip replacement sets off a metal detector at the airport.

Anonymous

STAYIN' ALIVE

I exercise every morning
without fail. One eyelid goes up
and the other follows.

Pete Postlethwaite

A gentleman is telling his friend about his new exercise regime: 'I think I'm a little old for all this gym stuff, but I'm building up some equipment at home. I got one of those Ab Roller contraptions recently. Thing is, I've been rolling it up and down my stomach for the past six weeks, and all I've got to show for it is this unsightly red line down my middle!'

Muscles come and go; flab lasts.

Bill Vaughan

It is better to wear out than to rust out.

Bishop Richard Cumberland

The best, the most exquisite automobile is a walking stick; and one of the finest things in life is going on a journey with it.

Robert Coates Holliday

'My doctor told me if I took up jogging it could add ten years to my life,' a middle-aged man was telling his friend. 'He was absolutely right – I now feel ten years older.'

… the dead centre of middle age… occurs when you are too young to take up golf and too old to rush to the net.

Franklin Adams

A determined lady of a certain age is telling a friend about her new aerobics class: 'I felt as if I was completely out of shape, so I just went for it. I stretched, twisted, jumped up and down and wiggled… Of course, by the time I'd got my leotard on, the class had finished.'

A man is standing on the bathroom scales desperately sucking his stomach in. 'That's not going to help,' says his wife. 'Yes it will,' replies the man. 'It's the only way I can see the numbers.'

A health specialist is giving a talk on well-being to an over-fifties club in the local village hall. 'The best way to start the day is to do five minutes of light exercise, and five minutes of deep breathing,' says the specialist. 'Then I take a hot shower, and feel rosy all over.' There are nods of agreement from the group until one wisecrack at the back pipes up: 'Tell us more about Rosie!'

Health nuts are going to feel stupid someday,
lying in hospitals dying of nothing.

Redd Foxx

How pleasant is the day when we give up
striving to be young – or slender.

William James

My doctor told me to do something that puts
me out of breath, so I've taken up
smoking again.

Jo Brand

It's no longer a question of staying healthy.
It's a question of finding a sickness you like.

Jackie Mason

An older woman goes to a leisure centre
and asks if she can join a gym class. 'I'm not
sure if that's a good idea,' says the instructor.
'How flexible are you?'
'Oh, very,' replies the woman. 'But I can't
make Tuesdays.'

HOLDING BACK THE YEARS

I don't plan to grow old
gracefully. I plan to have face-
lifts until my ears meet.

Rita Rudner

A sixty-year-old woman decides it's high time she had a facelift, so she goes for a consultation at a smart clinic. 'We have a new procedure,' the surgeon explains. 'We put a small screw in the top of your head, so that any time you see wrinkles reappearing, you simply turn the screw to tighten and lift the skin.' She thinks this sounds marvellous and signs up to the procedure that very day. However, the woman soon starts to experience problems and returns a few months later to give the surgeon a piece of her mind, 'This is the biggest mistake I've ever made! Just look at these terrible bags under my eyes!'

'Madam,' the surgeon replies, 'those are not bags, those are your breasts.'

There is still no cure for the common birthday.

John Glenn

I'm sixty-three now, but that's just
seventeen Celsius.

George Carlin

Age is not a particularly interesting subject.
Anyone can get old. All you have to do is live
long enough.

Groucho Marx

Looking fifty is great – if you're sixty.

Joan Rivers

I've found the secret of eternal youth. I lie about my age.

Bob Hope

Beautiful young people are accidents of nature, but beautiful old people are works of art.

Eleanor Roosevelt

I refuse to admit I'm more than fifty-two, even if that does make my sons illegitimate.

Nancy Astor

A traffic policeman stops a female motorist for speeding. 'Madam,' he begins, 'I'm sure you know exactly why I stopped you. As you came down the street I had you at sixty-five, minimum.'

'Outrageous!' the woman replies. 'I'm not a day over fifty-five. And besides, there's no way you could have made an accurate estimate – I was driving far too fast for that.'

The woman who tells her age is either too young to have anything to lose or too old to have anything to gain.

Chinese proverb

A diplomat is a man who always remembers a woman's birthday but never remembers her age.

Robert Frost

In dog years, I'm dead.

Anonymous

A woman's always younger than a man of equal years.

Elizabeth Barrett Browning

I do wish I could tell you my age but it's impossible. It keeps changing all the time.

Greer Garson

A lady goes into a cosmetics store and asks for a new anti-aging cream she has seen on TV. She spends the next month applying it day and night, but isn't sure if it's working or not. She decides to ask her husband: 'Darling, be honest, what age would you say I am?'

'Well,' he says, 'judging from your skin, I would say twenty; your hair, eighteen; your body, twenty-five.'

'Oh! You say all the right things,' she cries, covering him in kisses.

'Hang on,' the husband says, 'you didn't give me a chance to add them up!'

How old would you be if you didn't know how old you were?

Satchel Paige

There are three ages of man – youth, age, and
'You're looking wonderful.'

Francis Spellman

No man is ever old enough to know better.

Holbrook Jackson

No woman should ever be quite accurate
about her age. It looks so calculating.

Oscar Wilde

Jewellery takes people's minds off
your wrinkles.

Sonja Henie

A man who correctly guesses a woman's age
may be smart, but he's not very bright.

Lucille Ball

Men become much more attractive when they
start looking older. But it doesn't do much
for women, though we do have an advantage:
make-up.

Bette Davis

I must confess, I was born at a very early age.

Groucho Marx

I have never known a person to live to be one hundred and be remarkable for anything else.

Josh Billings

Whenever the talk turns to age, I say I am forty-nine plus VAT.

Lionel Blair

Old age is fifteen years older than I am.

Oliver Wendell Holmes

Time and tide wait for no man, but time always stands still for a woman of thirty.

Robert Frost

As a graduate of the Zsa Zsa Gabor School of creative mathematics, I honestly do not know how old I am.

Erma Bombeck

Age to women is like Kryptonite
to Superman.

Kathy Lette

Please don't retouch my wrinkles. It took me so long to earn them.

Anna Magnani

I don't believe in aging. I believe in forever altering one's aspect to the sun.

Virginia Woolf

Time may be a great healer, but it's a lousy beautician.

Anonymous

LOVE ME TENDER

An archaeologist is the best
husband any woman can have:
the older she gets, the more
interested he is in her.

Agatha Christie

After thirty years of marriage, a man looks at his wife one day and says, 'You know, thirty years ago we lived in a cheap apartment, drove a rusty old car and made do with a tiny twelve-inch TV set. Yet, every night I got to sleep with a hot twenty-five-year-old blonde.'

'Now,' he continues, 'we have a beautiful house, an expensive car, a big flat-screen TV, but I have to sleep with a fifty-five-year-old woman. It doesn't seem fair.'

'Well,' she snaps, 'why don't you go out and get yourself a hot twenty-five-year-old blonde? Then, once the divorce papers have gone through, you will be living in a cheap apartment, driving a rusty old car and watching a tiny twelve-inch TV set.'

A wedding anniversary is the celebration of love, trust, partnership, tolerance and tenacity. The order varies for any given year.

Paul Sweeney

A senior couple are sitting together watching television. During an advert showing a young, passionate couple the husband turns to his wife and asks, 'Whatever happened to our sexual relations?' After a long, thoughtful silence, the wife replies, 'You know, I'm not sure. Gordon completely forgot your birthday and we didn't even get a Christmas card from your sister this year!'

An older couple are planning their wedding, and before the big day they have a long conversation about how their marriage might work. They discuss the usual things like finances, living arrangements and so on. After some hesitation, the old man broaches the subject of sex. 'How do you feel about sex?' he asks hopefully. 'Well, I have to admit, at my age I like it infrequently,' she replies. The old man is silent for a moment and then asks, 'Sorry – was that one word or two?'

Two senior newly-weds are trying to get things started in the love-making department but they're not getting anywhere. 'You'll have to do something,' says the man. 'Like what?' asks his wife. 'You know,' he says, 'like moaning and stuff.' Thinking this is a reasonable idea, the woman begins: 'Would you look at the state of those curtains, they're hideous! And the dust on that dressing table! Didn't your mother teach you how to fold your trousers properly?'

I'd marry again if I found a man who had fifteen million dollars, would sign over half to me, and guarantee that he'd be dead within a year.

Bette Davis

Two men are pushing their trolleys around a hardware store when they collide. The older man says to the younger one, 'Sorry about that. I'm a little preoccupied – I can't find my wife, you see.' The young man says, 'That's OK. I'm looking for my wife too, actually. I can't find her and I'm getting a little desperate.'
'Well,' says the old man, 'two heads are better than one – let's help each other. What does your wife look like?'
'Well, she's twenty-four years old; blonde hair; blue eyes; she's wearing a short blue skirt... What does your wife look like?'
'Never mind,' the old man says excitedly, 'let's look for yours first!'

Never feel remorse for what you have
thought about your wife; she has thought
much worse things about you.

Jean Rostand

The concept of two people living together for
twenty-five years without a serious dispute
suggests a lack of spirit only to be admired
in sheep.

A. P. Herbert

A husband and wife are having a bitter
quarrel on the day of their ruby wedding
anniversary. The husband yells, 'When you
die, I'm getting you a headstone that reads,
"Here Lies My Wife – Cold as Ever".'
'Well,' the wife replies, 'When you die, I'm
getting you a headstone that reads, "Here
Lies My Husband – Stiff at Last".'

A man blows his retirement pay-out on a brand new BMW Z3 convertible. Turning on to the motorway, he decides to find out what his new toy can do. Just as he is pushing 120 mph, he sees the blue flashing lights of a police car behind him.

Rather than push his luck any further, he decides to pull over and take the wrap. 'Sir,' the policeman begins, 'my shift ends in ten minutes. Today is Friday and I'm going away for the weekend. If you can give me a reason why you were speeding that I've never heard before, I'll let you off with a warning.' The man looks very seriously at the policeman, and replies, 'Years ago, my wife ran off with a policeman. I thought you were bringing her back!'

I have learned that only two things are necessary to keep one's wife happy. First, let her think she's having her own way. And second, let her have it.

Lyndon B. Johnson

It used to be wine, women and song. Now, it's beer, the old lady and TV!

Anonymous

An old professor visits his doctor for a routine check-up and everything seems fine. The doctor proceeds to ask him about his sex life. 'Well,' the professor drawls, 'not bad at all, to be honest. The wife isn't all that interested any more, so I just cruise around. In the past week I have been able to pick up and bed at least three girls, none of whom were over thirty years old.'

'My goodness, and at your age too!' the doctor says with surprise. 'I hope you at least took some precautions.'

'Yep. I may be old, but I'm not senile yet. I gave them all a fake name.'

Tony is trying to persuade his wife, Alison, to go up in a plane at the local air show: 'But the ride is fifty pounds, and fifty pounds is fifty pounds,' argues Alison. Luckily for Tony, a pilot is walking past and overhears their argument.

He walks up to them and says, 'Listen, folks, I'll make you a deal. I'll take you both up for a ride. If you can stay quiet for the entire ride I won't charge you, but if you say one word it's fifty pounds!'

The couple agree to his terms and up they go. The pilot performs all kinds of rolls, twists and dives, and the couple remain absolutely silent. After a perfect landing, the pilot turns round to Tony and says, 'I'm impressed. I did everything I could think of to get you to yell out, but you didn't.' To which Tony replies, 'Well, I was going to say something when Alison fell out, but, after all, fifty pounds is fifty pounds!'

RELIGHT MY FIRE

At my age I'm envious of a
stiff wind.

Rodney Dangerfield

Two elderly men are talking about Viagra.
One has never heard of it and asks the other
what it is for. 'It's the greatest invention ever,'
he says. 'It makes you feel like a man of thirty.'
'Can you get it over the counter?'
'Probably – if you took four.'

A sixty-year-old man goes to the doctor's and
says: 'Doc, my sex drive is too high – I want it
lowered.' The doctor can't believe what he is
hearing. 'You're sixty and you want your sex
drive lowered?'
'That's right,' says the man pointing to his
head. 'It's all up here. I want it lowered.'

I once saw my grandparents have sex, and
that's why I don't eat raisins.

Zach Galifianakis

Everything that goes up must come down.
But there comes a time when not everything
that's down can come up.

George Burns

An old man goes to church to make a
confession. 'Father,' he begins, 'I'm sixty-
two years old. I've been married for forty
years. Until recently I had been faithful to my
wife, but yesterday I was intimate with an
eighteen-year-old model.' The priest replies,
'I see. And when was your last confession?'
The old man says, 'Actually, I've never been to
confession. I'm Jewish.'
'So, why are you telling me about this young
girl?' asks the priest.
'I'm not just telling you,' says the old man
excitedly, 'I'm telling everybody!'

An old lady is feeling lonely living on her own, so she decides to buy a pet to keep her company.

At the pet shop she stops to take a closer look at a frog, and to her surprise he whispers, 'Take me home and you won't be sorry.' So the old lady picks him up and gets into her car.

Driving down the road the frog whispers again to her, 'Kiss me and you won't be sorry.' The old lady thinks about this and says, 'Well, why not?'

So she stops the car and stoops down to kiss the frog. All of a sudden, in a blaze of fireworks and coloured smoke, the frog transforms into a handsome young man. The young man kisses the old lady in return, and you know what the old lady turned into? The first B & B she could find!

A man, getting on a bit, begins to find that he is unable to perform sexually. After trying everything conventional medicine has to offer, he decides to take a chance on a medicine man, who gives him a vial of blue liquid. 'This is powerful stuff,' the medicine man says. 'All you have to do is say "one-two-three" and you'll instantly rise to the occasion. When your partner is completely satisfied, all she has to say is "one-two-three-four", and the liquid will wear off.' The old gent rushes home, anxious to try out this new wonder potion. That night, he drinks the liquid, cuddles up to his wife and says 'one-two-three' and suddenly he's ready for action, just as the medicine man promised. Just then, his wife turns to him and asks, 'What did you say "one-two-three" for?'

When did my wild oats turn into shredded wheat?

Anonymous

A terrible thing happened to me last night
again – nothing.

Phyllis Diller

Two senior singles, Jack and Audrey, meet
at a dance one evening, and after several
weeks of going for coffees, decide to go out
for dinner on a proper date. They have a
lovely evening dining at the most romantic
restaurant in town, after which they go to his
place for a nightcap. Things continue along
a natural course and, age being no inhibitor,
Audrey soon joins Jack for a bit of rough and
tumble. Afterwards, as they both lie smiling,
they quietly ponder this special moment:
Jack thinks to himself: 'If I'd known she was
a virgin, I'd have been gentler.'
Audrey thinks: 'If I'd known he could still do
it, I'd have taken my tights off.'

A man is surprised to find his elderly father sitting on his deck chair in the garden, with no trousers on. 'What on earth are you doing sitting out here with no trousers on?' he asks. The old man looks at him slyly and says, 'Well, last week I sat out here with no shirt on and I got a stiff neck. This was your mother's idea!'

I can still enjoy sex at seventy-four. I live at seventy-five, so it's no distance.

Bob Monkhouse

Continental people have sex lives; the English have hot-water bottles.

George Mikes, *How to Be an Alien*

Two senior men are discussing the ups and downs of their sex lives: 'Did you know,' one says, 'that scientists have recently developed a soluble form of Viagra? I dropped one into my cuppa the other day.'

'Did it work?' the other man asks.

'Well,' the first man says, 'it didn't enhance my sexual performance, but it did stop my biscuit going soft!'

Two mature women are in a cafe talking. One says to the other, 'How's your husband holding up in bed these days?' The woman replies, 'To be honest, he makes me feel like an exercise bike. Each day he climbs on and starts puffing and panting, but we never seem to get anywhere.'

A noted sex therapist comes to the conclusion that people often lie about the frequency of their encounters, so he devises a test to tell how often someone has sex.

To prove his theory, he fills an auditorium with people, and asks each person in turn to smile. Using the size of the person's smile, the therapist is able to guess accurately until he comes to the last man in line, an elderly gentleman, who is grinning from ear to ear. 'Twice a day,' the therapist guesses. But the therapist is surprised when the man says no. 'Once a day, then?' Again the answer is no. 'Twice a week?' 'No.' 'Twice a month?' 'No.' The man finally says yes when the therapist asks 'Once a year?' Annoyed that his theory has been disproved, the therapist snaps, 'Then what on earth are you so happy about?' The gent answers, 'Tonight's the night!'

My best birth control now is to leave the lights on.

Joan Rivers

I only take Viagra when I'm with more than one woman.

Jack Nicholson

An old man goes to the doctor for his annual check-up. The doctor listens to his heart and pronounces: 'I'm afraid you have a serious heart murmur. Do you smoke at all?'
The man says no. 'Do you drink to excess?'
Again, the man says no. 'Do you still have a sex life?' the doctor asks. 'Yes,' the man replies. 'Well, I'm sorry to have to tell you,' the doctor says, 'but with this heart murmur, you'll have to give up half of your sex life.' Looking a bit perplexed, the old man answers, 'Which half – the looking or the thinking?'

OLD-FASHIONED ROMANCE

I'll see a beautiful girl walking up to me... I can't believe my good luck. But then she'll say, 'Where's your son?' or 'My mother loves you.'

James Caan

A mature man decides to throw caution
to the wind and approach a young female
library clerk he has taken a shine to. He goes
up to the counter and with a sly wink says,
'You know, some people say that when a
man reaches a certain maturity he becomes
attractive even to someone half his age…
have you ever heard that?'
'Yes,' she says, smiling brightly, 'as a matter of
fact I have. Fictional Romance, aisle four.'

You know you're over the hill when the only
whistles you get are from the tea kettle.

Raquel Welch

One of the best parts of growing older? You can flirt all you like since you've become harmless.

Liz Smith

Reg, a sixty-three-year-old postman, has worked hard all his life, never finding the time to get married. But one day a beautiful nineteen-year-old girl walks into his office and it is love at first sight. Within a month, Reg and Rachel get married and go to Butlins for their honeymoon. 'So how was it?' asks Bill, one of Reg's colleagues back at the post office. 'Oh, just beautiful,' replies a starry-eyed Reg. 'The cream teas, the karaoke... and we made love almost every night, we –'

'Just a minute,' interrupts Bill. 'At your age, forgive me for asking, you made love almost every night?'

'Oh yes,' says Reg, 'we almost made love Saturday, we almost made love Sunday...'

Old age is when a guy keeps turning off lights for economical rather than romantic reasons.

Anonymous

A senior couple are in a romantic mood. While the pair are wrapped up in bed the wife says, 'I remember when you used to kiss me every chance you could get.' So the husband leans over and gives her a little peck on the cheek. Then she says, 'I also remember how you used to hold my hand all the time.' So he reaches over and gently squeezes her hand. 'I can also remember when you used to nibble on my ear,' the wife says. The husband sighs, stands up, and starts to make his way out of the room. 'Where are you going?' asks the wife. 'To find my teeth,' says the husband.

An aging woman is telling her daughter about a date she has been on with a retired gentleman that she recently met. 'Can you believe I had to slap his face three times?' she says. 'What do you mean,' the daughter asks, 'did he get a little frisky?'
'Oh, no!' her mother explains, 'I had to slap him three times to keep the old bugger awake!'

Love is not a matter of counting the years...
but making the years count.

Michelle Amand

A widow and widower have been dating for about two years. After a happy courtship, the man decides to ask for the lady's hand in marriage. When he asks her, the lady is overjoyed and immediately says yes.
The next morning, he struggles to remember what her answer had been! He thinks to himself: 'Was she happy when I asked? I think so... but she did look at me funny.' After about an hour of trying to remember to no avail, he decides to give her a call. Embarrassed, he admits that he can't remember her answer to the marriage proposal. 'Oh,' she says, 'I'm so glad you called. You see, I remembered saying yes to someone, but I couldn't remember who I said it to!'

Men always want to be a woman's first love.
Women have a more subtle instinct: what
they like is to be a man's last romance.

Oscar Wilde

To keep the heart unwrinkled, to be hopeful,
kindly, cheerful, reverent that is to triumph
over old age.

Thomas B. Aldrich

[F]ood has taken the place of sex in my life...
I've just had a mirror put over my
kitchen table.

Rodney Dangerfield

A retired lady goes to visit her daughter and finds her naked, waiting for her husband Tim to return from work. The mother asks: 'What on earth are you doing with no clothes on?' To which the daughter replies shyly, 'Well, this is my "love dress" – I'm waiting for Tim to come home.' After the mother gets home she decides to strip naked and surprise her husband when he gets home. Upon arriving home, her husband asks, 'Dear, what are you doing with no clothes on?' With a smile she says, 'This is my "love dress" of course!' To which he replies, 'Well dear, I suggest you go and iron it.'

Two older women are watching their husbands from a bench as they wander through the park. 'Looks like your Edward still likes to chase the ladies,' one says, as she sees him greet a young girl he passes. 'It doesn't worry me,' the other says. 'Even if he could catch one he wouldn't be able to remember what he wanted them for!'

A couple of old chaps are taking a quiet stroll when they see a group of teenage girls. One says, 'You know, when I see pretty girls like that it makes me want to be thirty years older.'
'What?! Don't be daft,' says the other. You're sixty years old. If anything you should be wishing you were thirty years *younger*.'
'Maybe,' the other replies. 'But if I were thirty years older, I'd be past caring.'

A retired divorcee decides he needs a little romance in his life, and so goes out to try and find himself a girl.

After trying his luck at several of the seniors' dances and bingo nights, one evening he decides to stop off at a local pub. As he's commiserating with a pint he notices a young, shy-looking woman in the corner smiling at him. He decides to throw caution to the wind and ask if she'd like some company, to which she replies, yes. The man can't believe his luck, and as the night progresses they seem to be getting on like a house on fire.

As the pub is about to close, the woman invites him back to her place. They end up in the bedroom, when the man asks, 'So, did your mother tell you everything you need to know about spending the night with a man?'

'Oh, yes,' she replies. 'That's lucky,' the man says, 'because at my age you tend to forget these things!'

LAST INNINGS

I intend to live forever, or
die trying.

Groucho Marx

A senior lady is at her husband's funeral. She tells her daughter that throughout their married life they had enjoyed physical relations each and every Sunday morning in time to the church bells. 'Maybe he was getting a bit old for that sort of thing,' says the daughter. 'Nonsense,' replies the old lady. 'If it hadn't been for that ice cream van, he'd still be alive today.'

He is alive, but only in the sense that he can't be legally buried.

Geoffrey Madan

When doctors and undertakers meet, they always wink at each other.

W. C. Fields

The idea is to die young as late as possible.

Ashley Montagu

How young can you die of old age?

Steven Wright

George visits his solicitor to make a will. 'So what exactly do I do?' he asks.

'I'll just need you to answer a few questions, then you can leave it all to me,' says the solicitor. 'Well,' says George, 'I do thoroughly appreciate what you're doing for me, but I was hoping to leave at least some of it to my wife.'

My grandmother was a very tough woman. She buried three husbands and two of them were just napping.

Rita Rudner

Three elderly gentlemen are talking about what their grandchildren might say about them after they've passed on. 'I would like my grandchildren to say, "He was successful in business",' declares the first man. 'I want them to say, "He was a loyal family man",' says the second. Turning to the third gent, the first gent asks, 'So what do you want them to say about you in fifty years?'

'Me?' the third man replies. 'I want them all to say, "He certainly looks good for his age"!'

No one is so old as to think he cannot live one more year.

Marcus T. Cicero

I hope I never get so old I get religious.

Ingmar Bergman

I look at the obituary page. If my name is not on it, I get up.

Harry Hershfield on his morning routine

I don't think anyone should write their autobiography until after they're dead.

Samuel Goldwyn

DRIVING MISS DAISY

That's a good thing. He's getting old. He ran his entire last race with his left blinker on.

Jon Stewart on Mario Andretti's retirement from car racing

A group of ladies are chatting about their ailments over a cuppa. 'My arm is so weak I can hardly hold this teacup,' one complains. 'Yes, I know what you mean,' says another. 'My cataracts are so bad I can't see to pour the tea.'
'I can't turn my head because of the arthritis in my neck,' another friend says. 'My blood pressure pills make me feel faint.'
'I guess that's the price we pay for reaching our seventies,' one suggests.
'Well, it's not all bad... at least we're all still allowed to drive!'

If God wanted us to walk, he'd have given us pogo sticks instead of feet. Feet are made to fit car pedals.

Stirling Moss

The elderly don't drive that badly; they're just the only ones with time to do the speed limit.

Jason Love

A man is driving down the motorway when his mobile rings. It's his wife.
'Jack, drive carefully, I just heard on the news that there's a car going the wrong way on the motorway.'
'Tell me about it,' he replies. 'It's not just one, there are hundreds of them.'

While on a car trip, an elderly couple stop at the services for lunch. After finishing their meal, the woman absentmindedly leaves her glasses on the table, but she doesn't miss them until they are well into their journey.
'I'm sorry, Jim,' the wife says, 'but I've left my glasses at the service station. We'll have to go back for them.' The man fusses and complains all the way back to the restaurant, cursing his wife under his breath.
When they finally arrive at the restaurant, as the woman gets out of the car to retrieve her glasses, her husband says sheepishly, 'While you're in there, dear, you might as well get my hat, too.'

Oddly enough, all the bad drivers I've known
died peacefully in their beds.

Paul Johnson

I'm the worst driver... I should drive a hearse
and cut out the middleman.

Wendy Liebman

If you don't like the way I drive, stay off
the sidewalk!

Joan Rivers

An old lady is walking back to her car after doing the weekly shop at the supermarket. As she nears her car, she is shocked to find four strange-looking men sitting in it. She drops her shopping and draws a handgun from her bag and screams, 'Get out of my car this instant you scoundrels. I've got a gun!' The four men jump out of the car and run as fast as they can out of the car park.

After a few minutes of trying the key she realises that it doesn't fit... she gets out to see her own car parked five spaces down the row. Feeling overwhelmed with guilt, she drives to the nearest police station. As she's explaining her story to the sergeant at the station, he beings to giggle uncontrollably and points to the desk opposite, where four petrified men are telling another officer how they were car-jacked half an hour ago by a crazed old lady with a bobble hat and a .44 Magnum!

As you get older you need to sleep more. My favourite time is on the motorway, during rush hour.

Bob Hope

It finally happened. I got the GPS lady so confused, she said, 'In one-quarter mile, make a legal stop and ask directions.'

Robert Brault

I saw a second-hand car last week that was so old it had bifocal headlights.

Edward Philips

PARTIAL RECALL

Sometimes it's fun to sit in your garden and try to remember your dog's name.

Steve Martin

Two dear old friends of many years are playing cards, when one says: 'My friend, this is terrible, but can you remind me what your name is?'
Her friend gives her a long, hard stare, then replies: 'How soon do you need to know?'

First you forget names… Next you forget to pull your zipper up and finally, you forget to pull it down.

George Burns

Three things happen when you get to my age. First your memory starts to go and I've forgotten the other two.

Denis Healey

Those who cannot remember the past will spend a lot of time looking for their cars in mall parking lots.

Jay Trachman

It is lovely, when I forget all birthdays, including my own, to find that somebody remembers me.

Ellen Glasgow

The advantage of a bad memory is that one enjoys several times the same good things for the first time.

Friedrich Nietzsche

A well-dressed, debonair man in his eighties enters a swanky cocktail bar and finds a seat next to a good-looking, younger woman in her mid sixties, at the most. Trying to remember his best chat-up line, he says, 'So tell me, do I come here often?'

A senior lady calls 999 on her mobile phone to report that her car has been broken into. In a hysterical state, she describes the situation to the operator: 'They've stolen the steering wheel, the brake pedal and even the accelerator!' she cries. The operator tells her to keep calm, and that a police officer is on his way. A few minutes later, the officer reports back to the station. 'Disregard,' he says, 'She got in the back seat by mistake.'

Perhaps being old is having lighted rooms inside your head, and people in them, acting. People you know, yet can't quite name.

Philip Larkin

I have a photographic memory. Unfortunately, it no longer offers same-day service.

Anonymous

A retired couple go to dinner at the home of some old friends. After dinner, the two men get talking. One says, 'Last week we ate at a marvellous restaurant. I highly recommend it.' The second man says, 'Well, I'll take your word for it. What was it called?' The first man pauses, thinking intently, then says, 'What's the name of that flower you give to someone to be romantic, the one that is usually red that has thorns?'
'Oh, you mean a rose?' asks the second man. 'Yes, that's it,' says the first man. Then he calls into the kitchen, 'Rose, what's the name of that restaurant we went to last week?'

Old age puts more wrinkles in our minds than on our faces.

Michel de Montaigne

I'm a senior citizen and I think I am having the time of my life… Aren't I?

Anonymous

When you're getting old, there's no question in your mind that there's no question in your mind.

Anonymous

When it comes to staying young, a mind-lift beats a facelift any day.

Marty Bucella

A travel agent looks up from his desk to see an older couple at the window, peering inside at the posters showing the glamorous destinations around the world.

The agent, having reached his sales targets for the week and feeling a sudden wave of generosity come over him, decides to call the couple into the shop and says to them, 'I know that on your pension you could never hope to go on a luxury holiday, so I am sending you away at my expense – and I won't take no for an answer!' The couple are overjoyed, and within a week are on their way to an exotic, five-star resort.

About a month later, the lady returns to the shop. 'And how did you like your holiday?' he asks eagerly. 'The flight was exciting and the room was lovely,' she says. 'I've come to thank you. But, one thing is still puzzling me. Who was that old guy I had to share the room with?'

As you get older three things happen.
The first is your memory goes, and I can't
remember the other two...

Norman Wisdom

A man goes to his friends' home for
dinner. During the meal, he notices his
friend addressing his wife with endearing
nicknames, calling her 'honey', 'my love',
'sweetheart' and so on. While the wife is off
in the kitchen, the man says to his friend, 'I
think it's wonderful that after all these years
you still love your wife enough to call her
those pet names.' His friend hangs his head
and replies, 'To tell you the truth, it's because
I forgot her name about ten years ago.'

OLD FOLKS, AT HOME

We spend our lives on the run...
and then we retire. And what do
they give us? A bloody clock.

Dave Allen

Two retired professors are sitting on the
patio one fine evening, watching the sun set.
The history professor asks the psychology
professor, 'Have you read Marx?'
To which the professor of psychology replies,
'Yes, and I think it's these blasted
wicker chairs!'

As I get older, I just prefer to knit.

Tracey Ullman

Preparation for old age should begin not
later than one's teens. A life which is empty
of purpose until sixty-five will not suddenly
become filled on retirement.

Dwight L. Moody

The first sign of maturity is the discovery that the volume knob also turns to the left.

Jerry M. Wright

When you're a young man, Macbeth is a character part. When you're older, it's a straight part.

Laurence Olivier

I've got to watch myself these days. It's too exciting watching anyone else.

Bob Hope

When men reach their sixties and retire they go to pieces. Women just go right on cooking.

Gail Sheehy

At sixty-five, Jill decides she's ready to retire. At her leaving party at work her boss makes a speech: 'Well, Jill, there's no doubt that after you've left we'll find it hard to replace you... You could even say you are irreplaceable. Of course, that's mainly down to the fact that, for the past ten years, we're not entirely sure what it was you did around here!'

Getting old is a fascinating thing. The older you get, the older you want to get.

Keith Richards

People are living longer than ever before, a phenomenon undoubtedly made necessary by the thirty-year mortgage.

Doug Larson

A man of sixty has spent twenty years in bed
and over three years in eating.

Arnold Bennett

I can still cut the mustard... I just need help
opening the jar!

Anonymous

My parents didn't want to move to Florida,
but they turned sixty and that's the law.

Jerry Seinfeld

At his retirement presentation, Tom's boss decides to say a few words. 'We'd like to thank Tom for his many years of service to the company… I can say with absolute certainty that he's a man who, while at work, didn't know the meaning of "impossible task", who never took the words "lunch break" to heart, and who has shown professional contempt for the command "no". So, Tom, we've all clubbed together and bought you… a dictionary.'

Retirement at sixty-five is ridiculous. When I was sixty-five I still had pimples.

George Burns

I still have a full deck; I just shuffle slower now.

Anonymous

THE GIFT OF GRANDKIDS

Grandchildren don't make a man feel old; it's the knowledge that he's married to a grandmother.

Agatha Christie

A young mother's three-year-old son opens a birthday gift from his grandmother, and is delighted to discover that it's a water pistol. He heads straight for the nearest sink so he can fill it up. His mother, looking displeased, turns to her mother and says, 'I'm surprised at you getting him something like that. Don't you remember how we used to drive you up the wall with water guns?' At which the older lady smiles and then replies, 'Oh yes, I remember!'

Children are a great comfort in your old age – and they help you reach it faster, too.

Lionel Kauffman

Wrinkles are hereditary. Parents get them from their children.

Doris Day

An old lady visits her doctor and asks for some birth control pills. 'Why do you want them at your age?' asks the doctor. 'They help me sleep better,' replies the old lady. 'Oh, really? How?' asks the doctor. 'I put them in my teenage granddaughter's orange juice.'

'Nanny, nanny, I'm so glad to see you!' the little boy says to his grandmother 'Now Daddy will do the trick he's been promising us!'
'Oh?' His grandmother says, 'What trick is that?'
'He told mummy that he'd climb the walls the next time you came to visit,' says the little boy, grinning.

Blessed are the young, for they shall inherit the national debt.

Herbert Hoover

A young grandson decides to call his grandma and wish her happy birthday. While on the phone he asks, 'Grandma, how old are you now?' His grandma replies, 'I'm sixty-two years old now, son. It's been a long time coming.' After a slight pause, the grandson replies, 'Wow, Nan, that's a lot of years – did you start at one?'

What a bargain grandchildren are! I give them my loose change, and they give me a million dollars' worth of pleasure.

Gene Perret

The reason grandparents and grandchildren get along so well is that they have a common enemy!

Margaret Mead

A young girl is at the deli counter buying some food for her dinner party. 'I'd like five hundred grams of that cheese,' she says, 'two hundred grams of the smoked ham and – how much is the caviar, please?'

'It's quite expensive I'm afraid – fifty pounds an ounce,' says the smooth-looking male server, 'but from a gorgeous girl like you I'd accept a kiss for each ounce you buy.'

'OK,' the girl says after a little thought, 'I'll take five ounces.' With an excited look the male server quickly measures out the caviar, wraps it up and holds it out suggestively for the girl. As he does, the girl quickly snatches the food. 'Thanks,' she says, and points to an elderly man beside her. 'My granddad said he'd pay.'

AND ANOTHER THING...

Old age is an excellent time for outrage. My goal is to say or do at least one outrageous thing every week.

Maggie Kuhn

I have a problem about being nearly sixty: I keep waking up in the morning and thinking I'm thirty-one.

Elizabeth Janeway

If God had to give a woman wrinkles, He might at least have put them on the soles of her feet.

Ninon de L'Enclos

With sixty staring me in the face, I have developed inflammation of the sentence structure and a definite hardening of the paragraphs.

James Thurber

Audrey and Annabel are walking along the beachfront on a quiet Sunday afternoon, when all of a sudden a large seagull dropping lands on Audrey's shoulder. 'You see, Annabel,' she says angrily, 'this is why I don't come to the beach – too many undisciplined animals about! Do you have a tissue there dear, so I can sort this out?'

'Well, Audrey,' Annabel says, 'there doesn't seem to be much point – there's no way you'll get him to wipe his bum now, he's long gone!'

Inside every older person is a younger person – wondering what the hell happened.

Cora Harvey Armstrong

The surprising thing about young fools is how many survive to become old fools.

Doug Larson

By the time man is old enough
to read a woman like a book,
he's too old to start a library.

Anonymous

You can judge your age by the amount of
pain you feel when you come in contact with
a new idea.

Pearl S. Buck

Growing old is like being increasingly
penalised for a crime you have
not committed.

Anthony Powell

Women are not forgiven for aging. Bob
Redford's lines of distinction are my
old age wrinkles.

Jane Fonda

... at forty we don't care about what others think of us; at sixty we discover they haven't been thinking about us at all.

Anonymous

Nobody is forgotten when it is convenient to remember him.

Benjamin Disraeli

When you are younger you get blamed for crimes you never committed, and when you're older you begin to get credit for virtues you never possessed.

I. F. Stone

I've travelled a long way, and some of the roads weren't paved.

Anonymous

There's nothing worse than being an aging young person.

Richard Pryor

I would like to find a stew that will give me heartburn immediately, instead of at three o'clock in the morning.

John Barrymore

If I'd known how old I was going to be I'd have taken better care of myself.

Adolph Zukor

I'm fifty-nine and people call me middle-aged. How many 118-year-old men do you know?

Barry Cryer

Whatever poet, orator or sage may say of it, old age is still old age.

Sinclair Lewis

There was no respect for youth when I was young, and now that I am old, there is no respect for age – I missed it coming and going.

J. B. Priestley

A senior man and his wife are having an anniversary meal at Chez Trevor, a supposedly top-notch restaurant. As they're finishing their final course, the waiter comes over to ask them if they've enjoyed their evening. 'We would have enjoyed the evening,' the senior man begins, 'if the melon had been as cold as the soup, the soup as warm as the wine, the wine had been as old as the chicken.'
I'm so sorry, sir,' the waiter replies, 'is there anything I can do to make up for this?'
'As a matter of fact there is,' says the man. 'You can make the bill as cheap as the god-awful wallpaper you've got on the walls!'

The time to begin most things is ten years ago.

Mignon McLaughlin

By the time I have money to burn, my fire will have burnt out.

Anonymous

The first half of life consists of the capacity to enjoy without the chance; the last half consists of the chance without the capacity.

Mark Twain

You know you are getting old
when the candles cost more
than the cake.

Bob Hope

There is absolutely nothing to be said in favour of growing old. There ought to be legislation against it.

Patrick Moore

The older I get the better I used to be!

Lee Trevino

Youth would be an ideal state if it came a little later in life.

Herbert Asquith

The years between fifty and seventy are the hardest. You are always being asked to do more, and you are not yet decrepit enough to turn them down.

T. S. Eliot

Everything slows down with age, except the time it takes cake and ice cream to reach your hips.

John Wagner

... the sign of old age is that I begin to philosophise and ponder over problems which should not be my concern at all.

Jawaharlal Nehru

When our vices desert us, we flatter ourselves
that we are deserting our vices.

Francois Duc de La Rochefoucauld

I am old enough to see how little I have done
in so much time, and how much I have to do
in so little.

Sheila Kaye-Smith

The more you complain, the longer God lets
you live.

Anonymous

An old couple, bored of having tea at their regular restaurant, decide they'd like to experience a bit of modern cuisine.

So one night they head into the city and come across a trendy-looking restaurant – they walk in but are turned away as it's fully booked. 'I suggest, sir, that you call tomorrow to check if we've had any cancellations. You see, we're booked up for the next three weeks,' a haughty maître d' says. Feeling a little bemused, the couple return home.

The next evening they call the restaurant, but are told there have been no cancellations, and to try again another night.

After a week of calls, the old man has had enough and calls to complain: 'And let me give *you* some advice, sonny: trendy or not, you'd do a darn sight more business if you weren't so damn full all the time!'

KEEPING A TWINKLE
IN YOUR WRINKLE

It's sad to grow old, but nice
to ripen.

Brigitte Bardot

I love everything that's old: old friends, old times, old manners, old books, old wines.

Oliver Goldsmith

With mirth and laughter let old
wrinkles come.

William Shakespeare, *The Merchant of Venice*

None are so old as those who have
outlived enthusiasm.

Henry David Thoreau

The best thing about getting old is that all those things you couldn't have when you were young you no longer want.

L. S. McCandless

One of the good things about getting older is you find you're more interesting than most of the people you meet.

Lee Marvin

Another belief of mine: that everyone else my age is an adult, whereas I am merely in disguise.

Margaret Atwood

Two senior men, both dragging their legs slightly, pass each other in the street. One says to the other, 'I can see we've both discovered the perils of old age... what happened to you?' 'Well,' the other man replies, 'this is an old war wound coming back to haunt me. Took some shrapnel in the leg at Normandy, 'forty-four. What's your story?' 'Me?' says the other man, 'Got a problem with my foot. I trod in some dog muck a couple of streets back.'

You can't turn back the clock. But you can wind it up again.

Bonnie Prudden

I'll have a lot of wrinkles on my face, but I feel like my heart will be fat and full.

Goldie Hawn

I'm not denying my age, I'm embellishing my youth.

Tamara Reynolds

It's important to have a twinkle in your wrinkle.

Anonymous

I've only got one wrinkle and I'm sitting on it.

Jeanne Calment

I'm saving that rocker for the day when I feel as old as I really am.

Dwight D. Eisenhower

You're never too old to become younger.

Mae West

I was always taught to respect my elders and I've now reached the age when I don't have anybody to respect.

George Burns

Growing old is mandatory;
growing up is optional.

Chili Davis

Age is something that doesn't matter, unless <u>you</u> are a cheese.

Billie Burke

To get back my youth I would do anything in the world, except take exercise, get up early, or be respectable.

Oscar Wilde

You're not old. You're classic.

Anonymous

A man's only as old as the woman he feels.

Groucho Marx

Age is an issue of mind over matter. If you don't mind, it doesn't matter.

Mark Twain

There is no pleasure worth forgoing just for an extra three years in the geriatric ward.

John Mortimer

There is always a lot to be thankful for…
I'm sitting here thinking how nice it is that
wrinkles don't hurt.

Anonymous

A reporter is interviewing a group of senior
citizens for a newspaper feature entitled
'Super Seniors'. The reporter asks one lady
what the secret to her youthful appearance
is, to which she replies, 'I think a little bit of
everything is the best way to stay healthy and
happy. If you do things in moderation, you
can't go far wrong.'
'But madam,' the reporter replies, 'Your
daughter told us earlier that you have, on
several occasions, been seriously ill as a result
of your lifestyle.'
'Well, yes,' the woman replies. 'But you can't
very well put that in the article can you?'

Grow old with me! The best is yet to be.

Robert Browning

I don't want my wrinkles taken away – I don't want to look like everyone else.

Jane Fonda

I'm not interested in age. People who tell me their age are silly. You're as old as you feel.

Elizabeth Arden

The aging process has you
firmly in its grasp if you never
get the urge to throw
a snowball.

Doug Larson

Sometimes age succeeds, sometimes it fails. It depends on you.

Ravensara Noite

To be seventy years young is sometimes far more cheerful and hopeful than to be forty years old.

Oliver Wendell Holmes

I didn't get old on purpose, it just happened. If you're lucky, it could happen to you.

Andy Rooney

A man is not old as long as he is
seeking something.

Jean Rostand

Live your life and forget your age.

Norman Vincent Peale

He has a profound respect for old age.
Especially when it's bottled.

Gene Fowler

The trick is growing up without growing old.

Casey Stengel

After avoiding it for several years, a retired man decides to bring himself into the modern age and get a computer. His young grandson, a dab hand at using the Internet, decides to help him get to grips with surfing the World Wide Web. 'What's this search engine thing, then?' the old man asks. 'It's great, Granddad,' the grandson replies, 'you just ask it a question and it gives you the answer. You can find out anything!' 'Anything, eh?' the old man says, types 'What will next week's winning lottery numbers be?' and hits 'SEARCH'.

You're not over the hill until you hear your favourite songs in an elevator!

Anonymous

While there's snow on the roof, it doesn't
mean the fire has gone out in the furnace.

John G. Diefenbaker

I've got it two ways: I'm still making movies,
and I'm a senior citizen, so I can see myself at
half price.

George Burns

Don't act your age. Act like the inner young
person you have always been.

J. A. West

Cherish all your happy moments: they make
a fine cushion for old age.

Christopher Marley

As a senior citizen, you may as well learn to
laugh at yourself. Everyone else is.

Judy Huffman

Aging is a privilege, not a predicament.

Anonymous

There is no danger of developing eyestrain
from looking on the bright side of things.

Anonymous

A legend is an old man with a cane known
for what he used to do. I'm still doing it.

Miles Davis

There is no old age. There is, as there always
was, just you.

Carol Matthau

A WORD TO THE WIZENED

Wisdom doesn't necessarily come with age. Sometimes age just shows up all by itself.

Tom Wilson

Don't let aging get you down. It's too hard to get back up.

John Wagner

At a local cafe, a young woman is telling her friends about her idea of the perfect partner. 'The man I marry should be a shining light in company. He must be musical. Tell jokes. Entertain. And stay at home with me at night!' An old lady overhears and decides to speak up: 'Pardon me for saying so, but after a lifetime's experience I can say with confidence that if that's all you want, I would advise getting a TV!'

Old age is like everything else. To make a success of it, you've got to start young.

Fred Astaire

The gardener's rule applies to youth and age:
when young sow wild oats, but when old,
grow sage.

H. J. Byron

What is the most common remark made
by sixty-year-olds when they browse in an
antiques shop?
I remember these.

Old age... It is true you are gently shouldered
off the stage, but then you are given such a
comfortable front stall as spectator.

Jane Harrison

Age does not diminish the extreme
disappointment of having a scoop of ice
cream fall from the cone.

Jim Fiebig

A word to the wise ain't necessary – it's the
stupid ones that need the advice.

Bill Cosby

A woman past forty should make up her
mind to be young; not her face.

Billie Burke

Old age comes on suddenly, and not
gradually as is thought.

Emily Dickinson

An old man is walking past a group
of teenagers who are all laughing
uncontrollably. The man is intrigued and
so asks what the joke is. 'Well, if you must
know,' one boy explains, 'we're seeing who
can tell the biggest lie about their sex life.'
With a look of disgust the old man says, 'You
lot should be ashamed of yourselves! When I
was your age the thought of sex hadn't even
crossed my mind!' To which the boy replies,
'OK old timer, you win!'

The secret of staying young is to live honestly,
eat slowly and lie about your age.

Lucille Ball

Don't worry about avoiding temptation – as
you grow older, it starts avoiding you.

Anonymous

Middle age is when you go to bed at night
and hope you feel better in the morning. Old
age is when you go to bed at night and hope
you wake up in the morning.

Groucho Marx

Of course I have regrets, but if you are sixty
years old and you have no regrets then you
haven't lived.

Christy Moore

Anyone who stops learning is old, whether at twenty or eighty.

Henry Ford

Old age isn't so bad when you consider the alternative.

Maurice Chevalier

We are only young once. That is all society can stand.

Bob Bowen

An old-timer is someone who can remember
when a naughty child was taken to the
woodshed instead of to a psychiatrist.

David Greenberg

The key to successful aging is to pay as little
attention to it as possible.

Judith Regan

In spite of the cost of living, it's still popular.

Kathleen Norris

An old gent is backing his Rolls Royce into the last available parking space, when a young guy in a brand new sports car zips into the spot. The young driver jumps out and says, 'Sorry old boy, but you've got to be young and smart to do that.' The old man ignores the snide remark and keeps reversing until his Rolls crushes the back of the sports car into an unrecognisable mess. 'Sorry son, you've got to be old and rich to do that!'

You know you're getting old when you get to that one candle on the cake. It's like, 'See if you can blow this out.'

Jerry Seinfeld

… behave in a manner befitting one's age. If you are sixteen… try not to go bald.

Woody Allen

A person is always startled when he hears himself seriously called an old man for the first time.

Oliver Wendell Holmes

The best way to get most husbands to do something is to suggest that perhaps they're too old to do it.

Anne Bancroft

A man asks his father how he feels about reaching his sixty-fifth birthday. 'Well son, I've worked hard all my life, and to be honest, I don't feel like I've got much to show for it.' Seeing that his question had saddened the old man, the son decides to lighten the mood: 'But dad, what with the silver in your hair, the gold in your teeth and the gas in your stomach, you're worth a small fortune!'

Old age is like a plane flying through a storm. Once you're abroad, there's nothing you can do.

Golda Meir

True terror is to wake up one morning
and discover that your high school class is
running the country.

Kurt Vonnegut

Age is whatever you think it is. You are as old
as you think you are.

Muhammad Ali

There are people whose watch stops at a certain
hour and who remain permanently at that age.

Charles Augustin Sainte-Beuve

It takes a long time to become young.

Pablo Picasso

It's all that the young can do for the old, to shock them and keep them up to date.

George Bernard Shaw

They only name things after you when you're dead or really old.

George H. W. Bush

If you survive long enough,
you're revered – rather like an
old building.

Katherine Hepburn

Old men are fond of giving good advice, to console themselves for being no longer in a position to give bad examples.

Francois Duc de La Rochefoucauld

You must become an old man soon if you would be an old man long.

Roman proverb

The older I grow the more I distrust the familiar doctrine that age brings wisdom.

H. L. Mencken

I'm going to be eighty soon, and I guess the one thing that puzzles me most is how quick it got here.

Roy Acuff

Age is not different from earlier life as long as you're sitting down.

Malcolm Cowley

Old age is ready to undertake tasks that youth shirked because they would take too long.

W. Somerset Maugham

An inordinate passion for pleasure is the secret of remaining young.

Oscar Wilde

Forty is the old age of youth; fifty the youth
of old age.

Victor Hugo

We are always the same age inside.

Gertrude Stein

It is not how old you are, but how you
are old.

Marie Dressler

A concerned senior lady visits her doctor
to check her health. After her examination,
the doctor tells her that she's in good health.
'Good enough to live till a hundred?' she
asks. 'Well,' says the doctor, 'you don't smoke,
do you?'
'No,' she says. 'And you don't drink?' Again
the answer is no. 'And you don't have a
frivolous and excessive lifestyle, taking
advantage of every moment to
enjoy yourself?'
'Not at all,' the lady says. 'In that case,' the
doctor says, 'why on earth would you want to
live to a hundred?!'

The older you get, the more you tell it like it
used to be.

Anonymous

Old age ain't no place for sissies.

Bette Davis

You're only as young as the last time you
changed your mind.

Timothy Leary

If you think nobody cares if you're alive, try
missing a couple of car payments.

Flip Wilson

In three words I can sum up
everything I've learned about
life: it goes on.

Robert Frost

Have you enjoyed this book? If so, why not write a review on your favourite website?

Thanks very much for buying this Summersdale book.

www.summersdale.com